SPIDER

Garden Minibeasts UP CLOSE

John Woodward

CHELSEA CLUBHOUSE
An Imprint of Chelsea House Publishers

Spider

Chelsea Clubhouse
An imprint of Chelsea House
132 West 31st Street
New York, NY 10001

Library of Congress Cataloging-in-Publication Data
Woodward, John, 1954-
Spider / John Woodward.
p. cm. -- (Garden minibeasts up close)
ISBN 978-1-60413-895-5
1. Spiders--Juvenile literature. I. Title. II. Series: Woodward, John, 1954- Garden minibeasts up close.
QL458.4.W655 2010
595.4'4--dc22
2009040508

Chelsea Clubhouse books are available at special discounts when purchased in bulk quantities for businesses, associations, institutions, or sales promotions. Please call our Special Sales Department in New York at (212) 967-8800 or (800) 322-8755.

You can find Chelsea Clubhouse on the World Wide Web at http://www.chelseahouse.com

Produced for Chelsea House by Discovery Books
Managing Editor: Laura Durman
Project Editor: Colleen Ruck
Designer: Blink Media
Illustrators: Stuart Lafford and Tim Haywood

Photo acknowledgments: FLPA: pp 5 (Heidi and Hans-Juergen Koch), 9 (Mark Moffett), 26 (Imagebroker); Getty Images: p 29 (Maria Teljeiro); Photolibrary: p 16 (Oxford Scientific); Photoshot: pp 11 (Anthony Bannister), 19 (Stephen Dalton), 21 (Photo researchers), 22 (Stephen Dalton), 23 (James Carmichael Jr), 27 (Daniel Heuclin); Shutterstock Images: title page (orionmystery@flickr), pp 4 (3143818825), 7 (Audrey Snider-Bell), 8 (orionmystery@flickr), 10 (Cathy Keifer), 12 (Andrew Williams), 13 (Cathy Keifer), 17 (Natalie Jean), 18 (Sue Robinson), 20 (Cathy Keifer), 24 (Cathy Keifer), 25 (orionmystery@flickr)

Cover printed by Bang Printing, Brainerd, MN
Book printed and bound by Bang Printing, Brainerd, MN
Date printed April 2010
Printed in the United States of America

10 9 8 7 6 5 4 3 2 1

This book is printed on acid-free paper.

All links and Web addresses were checked and verified to be correct at the time of publication. Because of the dynamic nature of the Web, some addresses and links may have changed since publication and may no longer be valid.

Contents

Finding spiders

You can find spiders almost anywhere because they are amazingly common. There are probably thousands living in your backyard. Most of them are so tiny that you don't notice them.

This spider is making a web in someone's backyard.

Did You Know?

The extraordinary water spider (shown below right) spends most of its life underwater. It carries its air supply in a silvery layer around its body and lives in an air-filled bubble trapped in an underwater web.

Some spiders build webs among bushes and long grass. Their homes double as traps for their **prey**. Others hide in silk-lined burrows, or gaps between rocks and logs. Many more simply wander around on plants or on the ground. They do not have permanent homes.

A spider's body

You've probably seen lots of spiders in your home, garage, or backyard. The first thing you notice about a spider is its long legs. It has eight of them, which is two more than an insect has.

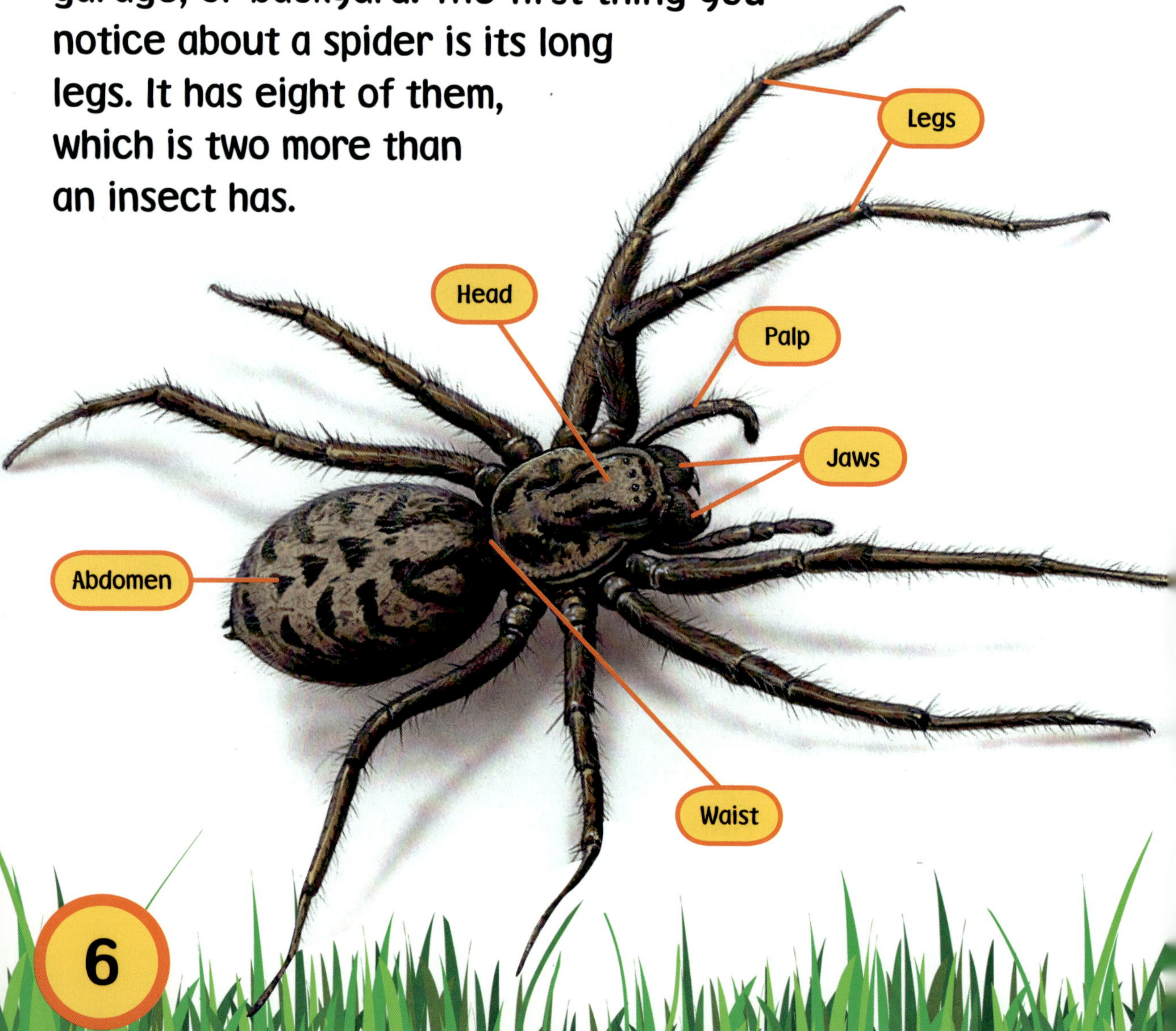

Did You Know?

The world's biggest spider is the South American goliath tarantula (shown above). It can have a legspan of ten inches! It is twice the size of the biggest spider in North America.

A spider's body is divided into two parts. The back part is called the **abdomen**. It is joined to the front part by a narrow waist. The spider's legs are attached to the front part, which is also its head. It has two feelers called **palps**, and a strong set of jaws.

Eyes and ears

Have you ever heard the expression "You've got eyes in the back of your head?" Well some spiders do have eyes all around their heads. Most spiders have eight of them. These are often very small. Spiders that trap their prey in webs are almost blind, but hunting spiders that chase after their prey can see quite well.

The little jumping spiders have especially big eyes, like car headlights. These give them very good vision.

Did You Know?

Spider eyes are quite different from the eyes of adult insects. In fact they are more like ours, although they have a lot more of them!

This web-weaving spider has small eyes on the top of its head.

A jumping spider has two big eyes and six smaller ones, including four at the side of its head.

Spiders also have sensitive bristles on their legs that work in a similar way to ears. These pick up tiny **vibrations** and air movements. They also have other sensors that pick up **scents** drifting in the air.

Venomous fangs

You might think that spiders are a bit scary or dangerous. However, most are quite harmless to humans. They are also useful because they eat insect pests like flies.

Did You Know?

Spiders do not need to eat much—they can often survive for months without any food at all.

This green lynx spider makes a meal of a fly.

The bristly, orange jaws of this wolf spider are tipped with sharp, black fangs. They pinch together to bite and inject venom.

Spiders have sharp, hollow **fangs** at the tips of their jaws that inject **venom** (poison) into their prey to kill it.

Then they must turn their food into liquid before they can swallow it. Some spiders do this by chewing their food and covering it with a liquid that turns it into a sort of soup. Flower spiders inject the juices into their victims and then suck them dry, leaving an empty shell.

Spider silk

Have you ever watched a spider making its silken web? All spiders produce silk. This is like a natural form of **nylon**, but more stretchy.

The web of an argiope spider has zigzag patterns of silk that may attract some insects.

The liquid silk is made by silk **glands** inside a spider's body. The glands are linked to **spinnerets** at its tail end. As the silk comes out of the spinnerets it instantly hardens into **fibers**. The spider pulls on these to draw them out, and the harder it pulls, the stronger the silk becomes.

Soft, strong silk is ideal for protecting this spider's eggs.

Did You Know?

The silk produced by tropical golden orb weaver spiders is the strongest known natural fiber. On some Pacific islands, local fishermen use the webs to catch fish!

Spiders use their silk to make protective cases for their eggs, soft nests for their young, and webs to trap their prey.

Orb weavers

Different spiders make different kinds of webs. Orb webs are deadly traps for flying insects such as flies. Many garden spiders use their silk to weave beautiful orb webs.

1

They often start by spinning a "dragline" that blows out on the breeze.

2

When the dragline catches on something the spider spins a second line.

3

The spider attaches another line to the middle. Then it drops down and pulls the web into a Y-shape.

4

The spider adds a lot more lines from the center. They look a bit like spokes on a wheel.

5

The spider links the lines with a rough **spiral**.

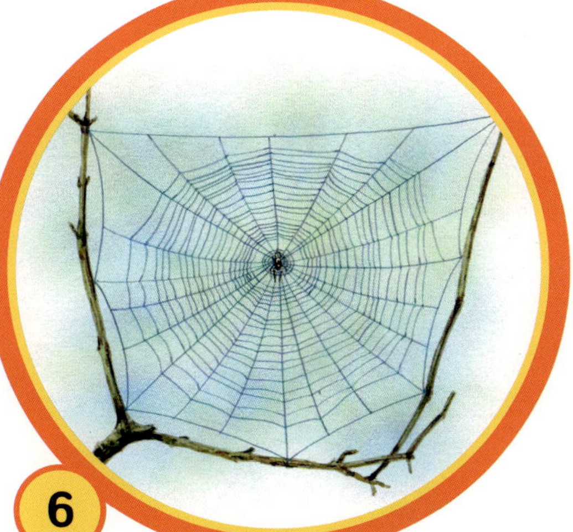

6

It then replaces this with a tighter spiral of sticky silk designed to catch insects.

Did You Know?

An orb weaver knows when it has caught a fly because the insect shakes the web as it struggles to get free. The spider rushes to the spot and wraps its victim in silk before killing it.

Traps and snares

Not all spiders make webs. Some lay hidden traps to catch their prey. The California trapdoor spider lives in a burrow hidden by a silk-hinged lid. If a passing insect strays too close, the spider flips up the trapdoor and darts out to drag its victim back into its burrow.

A California trapdoor spider lurks beneath its hinged trapdoor.

Did You Know?

A female ravine trapdoor spider of the southern United States can live for more than 12 years and spends nearly all that time in her burrow.

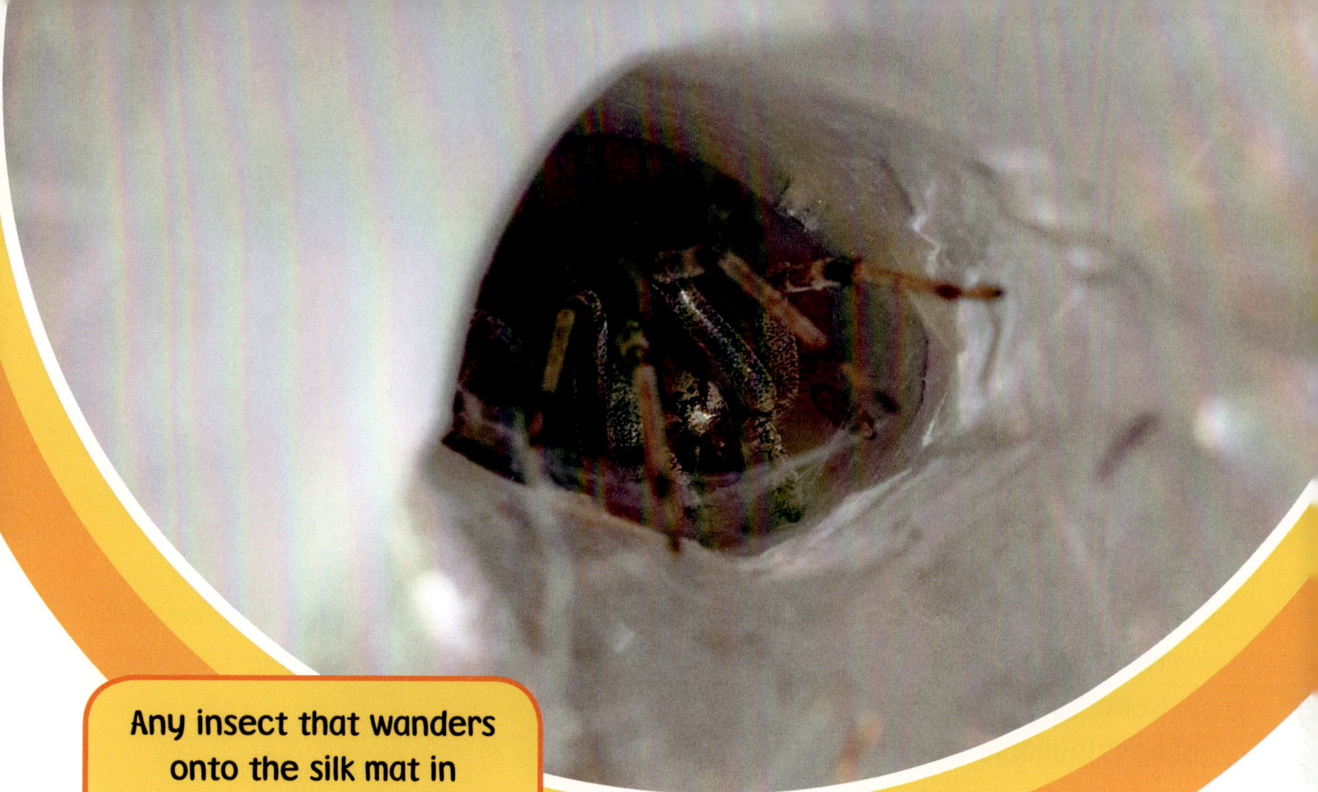

Any insect that wanders onto the silk mat in front of this funnel-web weaver's lair is in for a nasty shock!

Grassland funnel-web weavers spin large, flat webs called sheet webs. In the sheet web is an opening that leads to a silken funnel where the spider lives. When an insect disturbs the web, the spider senses this and rushes out to seize it.

Other spiders weave webs that look like hammocks supported by lines that go upwards and downwards. These entangle flying insects so they fall into the web.

Ambush killers

This honeybee has been seized by an almost invisible killer—a flower spider.

Some spiders are really sneaky. The common flower spider crouches in a flower waiting to seize **nectar**-feeding insects. They don't notice the spider because it can change color to match the petals! It catches the insect in its long front legs. Then it injects venom to kill its prey almost instantly.

Did You Know?

Some spiders fire sticky strands of poisonous glue at their victims, tying them down so they can't escape. They are called spitting spiders.

The bolas spider is even more cunning, giving off a scent that attracts moths. It spins a single strand of silk with a weight on the end and slings this at the moth to entangle and capture it.

A tiny spitting spider takes aim at a mosquito. These amazing spiders are common in homes.

Hunters and jumpers

Wolf spiders are fierce mini-hunters! They don't build webs or traps. Instead, they chase after their prey on the ground.

A wolf spider hunts among colorful fall leaves. Its big eyes watch out for insect prey.

Did You Know?

Big fishing spiders (right) that live on ponds can run across the water to catch prey. They are big enough to catch and kill small fish.

Lynx spiders hunt insects on bushes. They sometimes leap up to snatch flies out of the air. Jumping spiders are even more athletic, pouncing on their victims like cats catching mice.

All these hunters have very good eyesight compared to web weavers, which detect their prey mainly by touch.

Males and females

Did You Know?

During **courtship**, the male nursery-web spider offers the female a wrapped fly as a present to keep her happy.

Male spiders are much smaller than females, and some are so tiny it's hard to believe they are related.

A tiny male flower spider sits on the back of a female, who may not even know he's there!

A male has big "hands" on his palps that look like boxing gloves. In spring, male wolf spiders wave these at females in a courtship display.

Male orb weavers court females by twanging their webs in a special **code**, so the females know they are not insect prey. They must be careful, though, because the females might decide to eat them, anyway.

This male canopy jumping spider is performing his own version of the courtship dance.

Eggs and young

You may have seen little balls of silk in dark corners of your garage or basement. These are the egg **sacs** of female spiders. Many just leave these egg sacs somewhere safe, but the green lynx spider stands guard over hers. The nursery-web spider does the same, but also covers the egg sac with a dome-shaped web. When her babies hatch, they live inside the web.

Did You Know?

Many baby spiders travel long distances by spinning a thread of silk that catches the breeze and whisks them up into the air!

A mother green lynx spider builds her egg sac. She will guard it against enemies such as birds.

This mother wolf spider will carry her babies wherever she goes.

A female wolf spider carries her egg sac wherever she goes. When the eggs hatch she carries the tiny **spiderlings** on her back until they are big enough to take care of themselves.

Growing up

All spiders start life as tiny **replicas** of their parents. Orb weavers can even make their own miniature webs.

Baby spiders have hard skins like suits of **armor**. The only way a spider can grow is by **molting**, or replacing its old skin with a bigger one.

These baby nursery-web spiders are tiny compared to their mother, but they can soon take care of themselves.

A goliath tarantula gets rid of its old, brown skin so it can grow even bigger!

The spider pumps itself up to make the old skin split open, revealing a new, soft skin underneath. Then it hauls itself out and pumps blood under the new skin to stretch it before it hardens. It does this up to 15 times in its life.

Did You Know?

Molting is difficult for spiders, and they sometimes lose legs in the process. But this is no problem, because they can grow new ones!

Spiders and people

The black widow is quite small, with a red "hourglass" mark beneath her shiny, black body.

Many of us are scared of spiders, even though most are harmless. But some spiders are definitely dangerous.

The brown recluse spider's bite causes painful wounds that take months to heal. It sometimes gets into houses, so be careful!

The black widow also lives in garages and should be avoided. Its venom can stop people breathing, and some people have died after being bitten by this spider.

Spider bites are very rare, though. Most spiders cannot bite you, and even a black widow would rather run away from you if she can.

Did You Know?

The big, hairy desert tarantula looks dangerous, but it hardly ever bites and its venom is no more poisonous than a bee sting.

Most spiders are no threat at all, and some people even keep them as pets.

Glossary

abdomen: The soft-skinned, back part of a spider's body.

armor: A tough outer covering that protects the body.

code: A secret language that is understood only by those who know how it works.

courtship: Behavior used by a male or female to attract a mate.

fangs: Special teeth that, in spiders, are hollow and used to inject poison.

fibers: Thin single threads, like very thin fishing line.

glands: Structures in the body that produce special substances.

molting: Shedding a tough outer skin (or hair or feathers in other animals).

nectar: The scented, sugary fluid produced by flowers to attract animals such as bees.

nylon: A material that is very stretchy.

palps: Short armlike structures that a spider uses to feel its way around.

prey: An animal that is attacked and eaten by another animal.

replica: An exact copy that may be a different size.

sac: A baglike container designed to hold something, such as eggs.

scent: A strong smell.

spiderlings: Baby spiders.

spinnerets: The structures on the tail end of a spider that produce silk.

spiral: A curved line that starts in the middle and goes around and around, getting further away from the center.

venom: Any poison that is used by animals such as spiders, wasps, and some snakes to kill the animals that they hunt.

vibrations: Small, very fast movements that often make a sound such as buzzing.

Further resources

Books

Houghton, Gillian. *Spiders Inside and Out.* New York: Rosen Publishing, 2004.
Find out how spiders hunt their prey, eat, spin webs, reproduce, and lay their eggs.

McGavin, George C. *Amazing Insects and Spiders.* New York: Gareth Stevens Publishing, 2007.
Learn about the life cycles of some amazing insects and spiders.

Ross, Michael Elsohn. *Spiderology.* Minneapolis: Lerner Publications, 2000.
A close-up view of the world of spiders, including projects that help you learn more about how spiders live - and how scientists find out about them.

Solway, Andrew. *Deadly Spiders and Scorpions.* Chicago: Heinemann-Raintree, 2005.
A look at the really scary spiders such as black widows, tarantulas, funnel-web spiders, and their equally venomous close relatives the scorpions. Plus some other interesting spider facts. Only for the brave!

Solway, Andrew. *Spiders and Other Invertebrates.* Chicago: Heinemann-Raintree, 2007.
An investigation into the ways in which spiders have adapted to their surroundings to become successful, for example, in defending themselves and finding food.

Web sites

Backyard Nature, "Backyard Spiders," ***http://www.backyardnature.net/spiders.htm***
An interesting Web page containing information about spiders, and tips for spider watching.

University of Nebraska-Lincoln, Department of Entomology, "Spiders,"
http://entomology.unl.edu/images/spiders/spiders.htm
This Web site contains images of many common backyard spiders.

Explorit Science Center, "Spider Facts," ***http://www.explorit.org/science/spider.html***
A Web page of spider information from the Explorit Science Center in California.

Kidzone, "Spiders," ***http://www.kidzone.ws/lw/spiders/index.htm***
This Web page is full of information about spiders and has links to some online activities.

Tooter4Kids "Spiders," ***http://www.tooter4kids.com/Spiders/Spiders.htm***
A Web site full of information about spiders, with links to other spider Web pages.

Spiderz Rule, ***http://www.spiderzrule.com/spider7.htm***
This Web site contains photographs of spiders of the world. It has a clickable picture gallery giving access to information pages.

Index